Say It Well

Say It Well

Creating and Tailoring
Value -Driven Communication

Derek C. Lott

Foreword By:
Dennis Snipe

Conviction 2 Change LLC
www.conviction2change.com

Say It Well: Creating and Tailoring Value-Driven Communication by Derek C. Lott

Edition 2018

Published by Conviction 2 Change LLC
PO Box 47 Daly City, CA 94016
www.conviction2change.com

Library Congress Control Number: 2018955483
ISBN: 1732712107
ISBN-13: 978-1-7327121-0-2

Cover Design: Kayla Lott

Editors: Kayla Lott and Taylor D. Duckett

Table of Contents

Foreword

The desired outcome of any communication process (whether verbal, nonverbal or visualization) is understanding. Misunderstandings that result from miscommunications are a common, shared experience. Wouldn't it be awesome if we were able to successfully convey our thoughts, intents, and ideas to one another without the possibility of error?

In *Say It Well*, Derek Lott openly and honestly tackles many common questions and issues we have when it comes to speaking. For example: *What do I talk about? Will they listen to me? Will what I have to say be interesting?* We do not realize that each of us is full of information, stories and incredible content that would keep an audience captivated for hours! Yes, *you too!*

Derek also covers the proper use of your tools, using more words, taming the inner voice that says "nay" instead of "yay," and the importance of tailoring your content in a meaningful way so it is useful to other people.

As a broadcasting professional who has worked for over three decades in radio and television, I feel *Say*

It Well is masterfully written and guaranteed to increase your love for the spoken word and strengthen your ability to effectively deliver your message!

Dennis Snipe

Radio executive, talk show host, voice actor

www.dennissnipe.com

Introduction

Is there anything more important than communication? Throughout history our lasting accomplishments are marked by instances of new paths and great feats of communication. In the mid 1800's the need for fast communication inspired the Pony Express.[1] If you research that great moment in our history, you will find numerous accounts of what transpired. Let me give you the facts that are consistent story to story. It was extremely difficult to get mail from the Midwest to the West Coast. Three men developed a path that would enable 80 riders to make the journey and get mail from the Midwest to the West Coast in 10-15 days.

In that time, 10-15 days was considered a phenomenal accomplishment given it often took months for mail and communications to reach their destination. The Pony Express was a money-making

[1] The Pony Express was an innovative mail service that lasted 19 months and traveled 1,966 miles between Missouri and California.

endeavor. However, the mission of the financial endeavor was communication. The importance and value of receiving timely communication was a profitable consideration.

Interestingly, the Pony Express lasted fewer than two years. It was replaced by the telegraph—a faster form of communication. Think about our lives today. We have cell phones, the postal service, we text, we tweet, we snapchat and so on. Communication is an integral part of our society and being able to communicate well is my hope for you.

A recent report by Marriage.com highlighted lack of communication as one of the top ten reasons marriages fail. Communication is as important in the workplace as it is in your marriage. Effective communication is given such weight that there are dozens of great books on the market on the topic of speaking and communication. Traditional experts in communication like Dale Carnegie and newer authors like Carmine Gallo show us how to improve our presentations and share our thoughts with a captive audience. You can buy books about breathing techniques, creating the perfect PowerPoint®, and even books on what to wear when you present. I endeavor not to be redundant to these great resources.

Introduction

Say It Well: Creating and Tailoring Value-Driven Communication will teach you how to speak about what you know in a way that is true to your personality. You will also learn how to keep your message interesting and encouraging to your audience. As a business leader and an active member of the community, I have had many wonderful opportunities to communicate and present in high-stake situations. I remember having to present at work, and it never was easy, but I knew to further my career, it was essential. As you work through the lessons in this book, you will find many real-life examples from my own experience.

This book will help you discover, as I discovered, the unlimited content you have within you and teach you to use that content to connect with your audience. One of the most fulfilling parts of our journey in life is finding those who truly understand our values and passions. Many of us will spend our whole lives striving to find our place in the universe. It is important to be seen and heard in the way that we imagine ourselves. Whether you are a professional speaker, a recent college graduate, or someone who wants to be a better conversationalist, the ability to speak well is imperative to your way of life. The ability to communicate begins long before you even say a word.

I have two goals I strive to accomplish by the time you finish reading this book. First, to give you a process to develop content you can be confident presenting. Second, I want to help you use the tools you already have, along with your innate creativity, to tailor your content for any audience. You will be equipped to speak—on a big stage or at the neighborhood barbeque meeting new people. It all starts with the confidence that you have something to say, and that what you have to say is worth sharing with the world. Through the material in this book I will teach you the best way to communicate your stories and ideas with the people you want to influence. Soon you will be able to *Say It Well* each and every time the moment arises.

This book is meant to be a resource for your continued reference. As you review the Table of Contents, you can choose to read in a serial fashion or jump ahead topically to the area that aligns with what you most want to improve in your conversations. For example, if you feel you don't need help with the content piece, skip to the chapter on tailoring to learn how to create great connections with your listeners. The tips and lessons throughout will be useful to refer back to as you take the journey to be a better orator.

Introduction

Growing up my mom would tell me, *"If you can't say something nice, don't say anything at all."* She had a good point, but could have also added, *If you can't say something interesting or of value, don't say anything at all.* Your reputation is often built on what others receive from you, whether tangible or intangible. Be sure when you bring a thought or idea to a conversation, it adds something of value to those listening.

Idle chit chat may be good with a close friend or when you are alone pondering what you'll eat for dinner. However, in a large auditorium where people have traveled a great distance or paid to listen, they are expecting to obtain value from their time with the speaker. Similarly, a person whose attention you have sparked may indicate they are interested by leaning closer if they want to hear more. Coming up with something to say is not always easy. Don't underestimate the importance of meeting your listeners' expectations to keep their interest in what you have to say. How often have you been in a conversation and the other person is talking and talking and you find your mind wandering to what's for dinner or what am I going to do this weekend? You are brought back to reality when they snap their fingers at you and ask if you have heard a word that they have just said. You have drifted off so far that you have left the conscious world for a far more enjoyable unconscious one. It is far worse when you are in church or at a conference, and the speaker isn't holding your attention, so you tune them out. In this instance, there is no snap of accountability to bring you back. You find yourself either totally tuned out or getting a quick 20-minute power nap.

You can *Say It Well* with much more than idle chit chat, and I will show you how to take the first steps to becoming a better communicator. As you move forward, I leave you with a fable:

> *A dog jumped over a wall to chase a cat who jumped over a fence to chase a mouse who ran into a hole. Why? That's what they do. The owner of the land felt sorry for the dog and for the cat, because every time the dog would jump over the wall to chase the cat that jumped over the fence, the dog's paw would get caught in the fence. And every time the cat would jump over the fence to chase the mouse that ran into a hole, the cat's paw would get caught in the hole. So, the owner of the land plugged the hole, knocked down the fence and tore down the wall. The*

next day the dog sat down, the cat lay around, and the mouse had nowhere to go.

After a few days the dog, the cat, and the mouse began to wail. The wife of the owner of the land grabbed the shotgun off the wall to shoot the dog, the cat, and the mouse. The owner intervened and said he would take care of it. Within the day, the man unplugged the hole, raised the fence and rebuilt the wall. The next day the dog jumped over the wall to chase a cat that jumped over the fence to chase a mouse that ran into a hole.

What is the moral of the story? The owner of the land felt sorry for the dog and the cat because they never got the prize. The dog never caught the cat and the cat never caught the mouse. What the owner did not know is that each day the dog, the cat and the mouse woke up with vigor and vitality for the hope of the prize. It was the journey that they cherished. This book is not meant to be your prize, but rather the challenge on your journey in hope of the real prize: to *Say It Well.*

Chapter 1

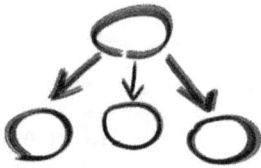

Create Endless Content

"The creation of a thousand forests is in one acorn."
-    *Ralph Waldo Emerson*

In my early experiences speaking to groups, I often had trouble determining what to talk about. It wouldn't be honest of me if I said I wasn't nervous. The bigger challenge was associated with having something to say and saying something of value. What should I talk about? How can I come up with something interesting enough to engage this group of people? I knew I wanted to send them away feeling challenged and inspired to carry out the task at hand. What could I say that would produce this outcome?

My biggest learning curve came from communicating with my team in my early days as a manager. I primarily used one-on-one communication with my team to avoid larger settings. However, to ensure the team operated effectively, I needed to start to communicate to the larger group. The first time I addressed the group collectively, I was extremely nervous. I knew what I wanted to say, but the words weren't coming. It was like the cat had a hold of my tongue. All my fears and insecurities were racing through my mind as I tried to gather my thoughts. I communicated something to my quiet audience and at the end, there were no questions . . . thank God!

However, I found out later that I didn't do a very good job. No one in my team was sure of what was expected, but they didn't ask any questions. Rather than their silence being a sign of understanding, I found out my captive audience did not ask questions because they did not want me to be offended at the lack of valuable content. My speech didn't add any value to the way they were doing their jobs. This was important for me to learn early on. I continued to work on my communication with the team and over time we reached a great rapport as well as desired results.

My intent in writing this book is to help you communicate clearly and make sure you never run out of content. If you are going to be successful at speaking, you must have something of value to talk about. In Chapter 5, I will explain how to connect that content to your audience. A deep connection with your audience is where you can start to see great personal satisfaction and rewards from having great content. I believe that every one of us has an endless reservoir of content. I know what you are thinking, *the guy that could barely come up with two words to say at the office is going to convince you that you have endless content within you.* Have a little faith, apply the following steps to begin building content, and you will be well served.

YOU are the key to creating endless content.

You are the key to creating endless content, and what's even more exciting is that you are already an expert on the topic of you. This means you don't have to spend hours researching what to share about yourself; you have lived it. In most situations, and with very limited preparation, you have what you need to speak about yourself at a moment's notice. We all have topics we could talk about ad nauseum. We just don't think about it every day.

Developing conversation around ourselves can help open the blocks we have when coming up with things to talk about. Whenever you entreat someone to tell you about themselves, they light up and are thrilled. When someone gets going about a topic they are passionate about (in this case their own experiences), often you can't quiet them. The joy we have in talking about ourselves may only be outmatched by talking about our children.

How many of us come from a family? Yeah, that's most of us. Whether it's good or bad, we all came from somewhere. Your family is a well of content. However, to be able to mine the content from this subject area, we will need to dig deeper.

Grab a pen and do the following exercise with me. You will be creating a Tree of Content, or what I call TOC. Take out a piece of paper and draw a circle and write YOU in the center of the circle at the top of the page. Then draw a branch from the circle with the word FAMILY inside. Talking about family is very broad, so I want you to begin to write several branches off family. Let's write Mom, Dad, Brother, Sister, Grandmother, Grandfather, Uncle, Aunt, Cousins, as many of these as apply to your family.

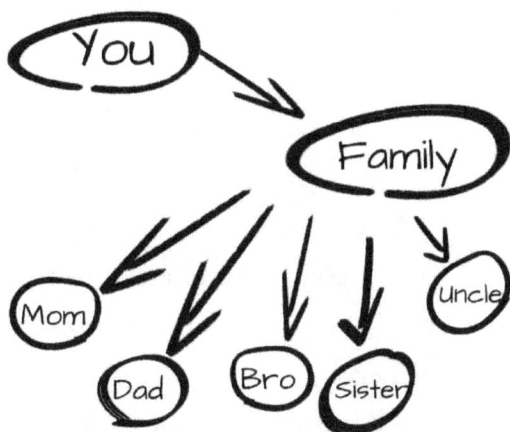

The point of this exercise is to branch from YOU in one area of your life. I call this activity treeing or branching. As you continue, the next levels down are where the topics get really interesting. Let's say your mom was a disciplinarian. You can draw a branch off the circle with your mom that says disciplinarian. You may recall several stories from your childhood that stand out and would be great stories to share with listeners. You may have an eccentric uncle (I think we all do) who tells great stories about sports or fishing trips, etc. All these facets of knowledge and experiences are pre-packaged content ready to be delivered to your audience.

Family isn't the only branch we could write from YOU.

We could talk about your career. We could talk about your hobbies, your relationships, or any of your other main interests. These broad categories are just a drop on the surface of a pool of endless content, the proverbial tip of the iceberg. I remember my first revelation that I had an endless reservoir of content within me. I was on a short plane ride, and I was inspired to start branching. At the end of the two-hour plane ride, I had over 200 branches.

I tried the exercise with a friend and really had a hard time getting the first topics on the board because I was only guessing at the topics, they were interested in. Once I started asking questions and actively listening to their answers, we started to make some progress. What hobbies do you have? What do you do when you unwind at home? My friend mentioned they liked to read. I said let's build a tree on the best reads you have encountered over the last few years. She remembered several that she enjoyed immensely and would love to share with others.

After some more discussion, I was able to suggest that my friend group the dozens of her favorite books by genre:

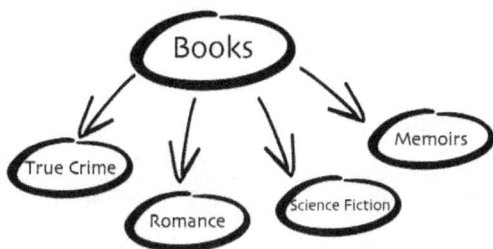

The types of books my friend liked to read let them really dive into the different series and authors she enjoyed. You might be thinking, *when can I bring up books to read?* Why would someone talk about books and reading for a given length of time? It is useful to have a way to talk about your own interests so that you can find common ground in new situations.

Communicating your interests is a way to connect with people so you can begin to find common ground.

Let's use the example of my friend. She likes to read after work because she enjoys unwinding in the evening with a book and a glass of wine. She may be invited to a social event where they do not know a lot of people. Small talk is a common way to break the ice. Someone asks, *"What do you like to do?"* or some variation thereof. My friend can answer intelligently about their own preferences while bringing the conversation back to the other person.

What are some topics you could speak or write about?

Think about the topics I mentioned in the beginning. Even branching off from the topic of family, I can speak at length about who is in my family, our traditions, quirky stories, etc. A simple way to start is below:

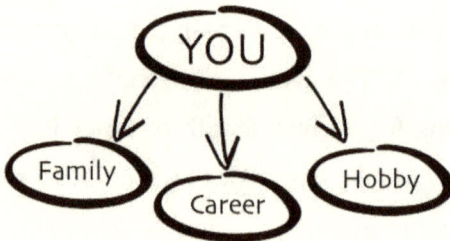

I hope this gives you a good base for the types of topics, relationships and interests that are in your universe. The next step is to take each one of these items and build the depth of the branches.

During a presentation on the topic of endless content, I demonstrated this technique live with the help of an unassuming audience member. I had never used this technique live before and I wanted to put my money where my mouth was. I had a person come up on stage and draw the initial circle with YOU in it.

Then we wrote family, career, hobby, etc., as it applied to her specific circumstances. I asked her about one of her hobbies, and she said she was into archaeology. I said that is interesting and invited her to tell me more about this hobby. The chosen audience member mentioned several topics and techniques. I explained she could give several speeches or have great conversations focusing on the many facets of archaeology.

Interestingly, I never knew this much about archaeology and many in the audience didn't either. The audience member was adding value to our lives because we were learning something new. She was so passionate about the subject that she began to explain facets such as the fact that there are historic, prehistoric, underwater and classical archaeology fields.

Once she broke it down, it was clear that she could have a conversation at length about some of the misconceptions of archaeology as well. Though often confused with geology and paleontology, archaeology is concerned with cultural norms of civilizations of the past. The audience was fascinated, as was I, and it proved my point that we all have something to talk about. My final point in my speech was to explain that just on this area alone, the audience member could develop several speeches or short conversations.

With enough preparation, she could deliver a keynote on archaeology that would be quite intriguing. The audience was fascinated to hear her unprepared remarks and she explained her knowledge and ideas with grace and poise. The audience member was beaming by the end and I noticed several people approach her for more information. The TOC on the next page starts to delve into the main points of archaeology and can provide endless content.

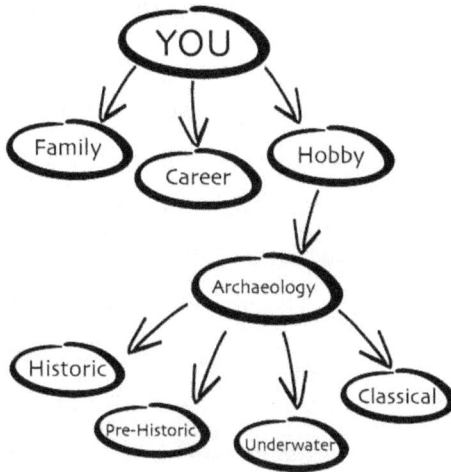

Another gentleman mentioned his hobby was doing woodworking projects in his garage. I asked him if he worked on large cabinets. He said no, that he primarily focused on wood carving. Again, very interesting and extremely educational. People love to learn things that they know nothing about, even if there is only time for a cursory overview. Specific information, especially when given by a passionate expert, adds value because it creates a way for the audience to try learning about a new topic without having to make an investment in equipment or materials. It brings the conversation to another level when we learn a useful nugget or pick up a fresh perspective. It adds to our life. The content that is in you is valuable to someone, if you share it.

The true-to-life people that I have helped over the years during one-on-one conversations or seminars reinforce for participants that they are interesting and have something to say and that the wider world is interested in their message. The most important point here is that much of what people talk about everyday pulls from life experience. They are talking from their core experiences, either personal or professional, and the research has already been done in the course of living it.

The work has already been done, you lived it.
Now tell it.

Talk about your job, the crazy boss on your job, or the really nice one.

Talk about your kids.

Talk about exotic trips you've taken.

Talk about your fears and phobias.

Talk about your hobbies (one at a time please).

Talk about your mom, your dad, your grandma or your grandpa.

Talk about your dog, cat or maybe you have a non-traditional pet.

Talk about your worst vacation ever.

Talk about dinner at your house, your favorite foods.

Talk about your first car, maybe you still have it.

Talk about your first date, that blind date.

Your experiences will remain only your experiences until you share them with others to further your story.

Speaking about yourself to others can decrease some of the initial fear of speaking as you are more likely to be comfortable with the content that you have learned during your life. Preparation can be intimidating, but when you have the content already living inside your head and your heart, it only has to be brought back to your recall for you to present in a competent manner.

Your memories are valuable but beware; they can also deceive you. Often our experiences are remembered through the lens of our current emotional state. If you look on a memory with disdain or embarrassment you will be tempted to share only the portion of the experience that you are comfortable sharing. The most effective communications are transparent; to do otherwise limits the value that the listener can receive from the discussion. This can limit transparency and stilt your communication before you even begin.

You have to share it all, as best you can, without filtering to show yourself in a more favorable light. We all have that "knower" inside of us that can sniff out a phony or someone who is hiding something. Being disingenuous will discredit you faster than outright lying. If you are not willing to tell it all, do not share that specific story. One way to organize your ideas would be when you are building your TOC, you can highlight sensitive subject matter with a symbol to remind you to keep those stories for when they no longer bring you discomfort.

The ability to be transparent and vulnerable is part of what makes the difference between good and great and makes great speakers and conversationalists so compelling. They give it their all and powerfully share their experiences—the good, the bad, and the ugly. Great speakers don't hold back anything; many become emotional or have the power to move the crowd to tears.

Jimmy Valvano, the great NC State coach, said:

When people say to me how do you get through life or each day, it's the same thing. To me, there are three things we all should do every day. We should do this every day of our lives. Number one is laugh. You should laugh every day. Number two is think. You should spend some time in thought. Number three is, you should have your emotions moved to tears, could be happiness or joy. But think about it. If you laugh, you think, and you cry, that's a full day. That's a heck of a day. You do that seven days a week, you're going to have something special (Valvano, 1993).[2]

Moving others to emotion is adding value and makes a difference in their lives. As you build your tree of topics and experiences, you can be free to help others and yourself by sharing the whole of your story. Don't let your concern over what others may think restrict your story. If you are not willing to be open, you will hinder your effectiveness.

One thing a listener can sense is authenticity

---

[2] Taken from Coach Jimmy Valvano's 1993 ESPY Awards Speech.

or the lack thereof. They can perceive when you are leaving out important information or a key part of the story. The work that you have put into sharing with that audience will be lost due to your lack of candor. *What are you protecting? Why are you there? Are you there for them or for yourself?* Remember: there is nothing to be ashamed of or embarrassed about. You and your story are good enough without defaulting to embellishments or half-truths.

Advanced Use of Your Tree of Content (TOC)

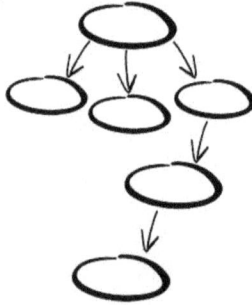

Now that you have started building your content, let me share an advanced tip about how to use the branches of your TOC to time your speeches. In my experience, you can create five to ten minutes of continuous monologue for each leaf on a branch.

The deeper the branch on any given topic, the more content you can create around it. Let's say at the deepest point of a branch you are four levels deep. That level represents 40 minutes of potential conversation. You are well on your way to developing a keynote of 30 minutes to an hour because of the depth of your knowledge regarding that specific topic. Refer to your tree often and continue brainstorming content. You will come up with new topics to brainstorm around and can add branches to your tree. This occurs when you pick up a new hobby or interest. This also occurs when a new relationship or family addition begins. Your story is constantly being written and rewritten each and every day. Continue the process of developing your tree, and you will see that you are a reservoir of endless content.

Stuck on a branch?

You can always begin a new TOC with a clean sheet of paper.

Chapter 2

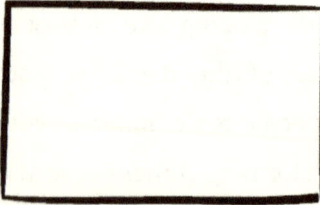

Organize Your Content for Instant Usage

"First comes thought; then organization of that thought, into ideas and plans; then transformation of those plans into reality. The beginning, as you will observe, is in your imagination."

- *Napoleon Hill*

When my kids were young, I helped them organize their thoughts for writing essays assigned for school. I taught them to create an outline for their papers and advised them not to write anything until they could tell me the gist of their paper by solely reading the outline. They often would become frustrated with me when I would ask them to repeat and refine the topics. The purpose of creating an outline, and the reason why I was so strict with my kids is to have a strong foundation to build content upon. The outline for your content is the frame to hang your speech on.

In Chapter 1, you built a Tree of Content. In this chapter, I will show you a simple method to organize your ideas, so you can quickly and easily use them. The tool I like to use for organizing my content is a simple 5x7 index card.

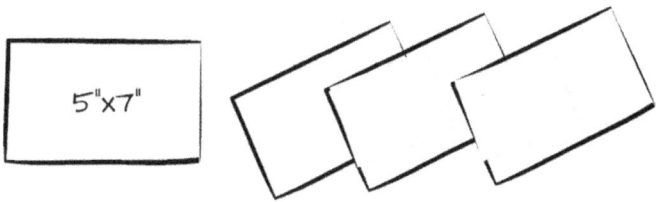

I keep a stack of blank index cards in my car and another set at my desk at work. Whenever a particularly interesting thought crosses my mind, I write it down. One topic or quote per notecard. The notecard system is a great way to keep from getting overwhelmed when planning what to say. Grouping index cards by subject can help you create a longer version of the content you had in mind.

With this start, take your endless content and organize it into usable notes that can be referred to very quickly. These will help you effortlessly prepare to deliver a great message to your audience. It is commonly taught that you should refrain from memorizing speeches because it can cause problems if you forget where you are or lose your place. The preferred method is to have points and write those points down, so you can reference them if needed. I find that index cards are perfect for this purpose. The method I outlined at the beginning of this chapter is extremely effective when you know the content. Knowing the content is easy and easily recalled when it is based on your experiences, your thoughts and your journeys.

The first step is to create an introduction.

Compile a couple of sentences that grab the listener's attention; then speak to what your topic is all about. For the outline, you are not writing a full introduction; just the key information for you to set in your opening thoughts in your mind.

A quote is a great way to start a conversation because it gives you shared credibility with the person you are quoting. You can follow it with a sentence explaining what you're going to cover and why it is important. Depending on the purpose and intended audience of your speech or communication, you can choose a famous person with a well-known quote, or you can include a quote from someone dear to you or personally known by the listeners. A great way to look up quotes on any topic is to do a quick Google search and find a quote that fits the intended tone. Be cautious when pulling quotes from online sources; make sure to check the validity of the credited author so you don't accidentally misquote someone.

Quotes are not reserved only for formal presentations or motivational speeches. I have used quotes in many settings, and I believe they are just as powerful in a one-on-one conversation as on a stage. We need to make sure we are not trying to sound pretentious, but people love learning from and being inspired by great people and what they had to contribute to our human family.

I want you to consider two versions of an introduction for the same speech:

Version 1

> *"Far better it is to dare mighty things, to win glorious triumphs, even though checkered by failure, then to rank with those poor spirits who neither enjoy much nor suffer much, because they live in*

that grey twilight that knows neither victory nor defeat." Tonight, I would like to bring this famous quote by Theodore Roosevelt to life and talk to you about taking chances and how to succeed even when you fail. My goal will be to convince you that you have the skills and the resources no matter what your personal circumstances are. The question is: do you believe in yourself enough to work hard to take what you want?

Version 2

My mother used to say, "You can't always get it right, but you can't give up." Have you ever felt that way? I hope you have something and someone to believe in because that will keep you motivated to never quit until you achieve your goals, just like my mother's words kept me.

Version 1 is more formal, suited for a larger audience, and requires more effort to memorize the quote. Version 2 is ready for a shorter speech or an informal setting and lends itself to easy recall.

Pretty simple right? The key is to be disciplined and descriptive, two or three sentences. That will make memorizing your introduction easier, ensuring you are fully loaded to deliver a powerful message. To be sure you will enhance your message when you are with your audience, you may add that you loved your mother for all her sayings, but one sticks with you, and you find yourself often referring to it. You may talk about the year that you failed, were disappointed by your lack of success, and how that led you to work harder and discover what it takes to be successful. The beauty of the introduction in your outline is that you can simply choose to stick to your two to three sentences, and that will always be extremely effective.

The next step is to define three descriptive points that will support your topic—these points will trigger your memory.

Three is a simple number set of information to grasp. These points need to grab and hold your audience's attention. You need to make sure people want to connect with these points. Avoid the clichés too often sung that people have heard hundreds of times before. If your points tend to lean in this direction, be creative. Spin them in a way that you have never heard before.

At a church event, I heard a guest speaker say fear is not a stop sign. That statement was revolutionary to me, it changed me. I had never heard it put that way before. We have all heard Franklin Delano Roosevelt's quote, *"There is nothing to fear but fear itself,"* and Napoleon Hill's, *"Fears are nothing more than a state of mind."* Both men made memorable points but because the notion of fear was approached differently by this speaker, I was completely captivated and yearned to hear more.

Spend a fair amount of time thinking about your points. You may have a single captive listener, or a full audience who have made an investment to come and spend time engaging with you. Your listeners will appreciate your preparation and feel that you are bringing value to the dialogue. They want to learn something and have takeaways to share the next day at work, with co-workers or at home with family and friends. Make sure you have put your message together in a way that will educate the listener, add value to their lives, and give them a novelty, new philosophy or do differently.

If you are conveying a personal story or humorous event, think about the stories that will move the audience or drive an emotional connection. I am convinced that a story is the best way to deliver any message to an audience. So much so, in fact, that I have dedicated a chapter to storytelling later in the book. I was at a speech contest not too long ago and heard a man tell a story about a mother that wrote the names of the children in their peanut butter sandwiches. On one occasion one of the children broke a favorite vase or keepsake. The mother wrote I forgive you in the peanut butter message. Now that was great, and the speaker delivered the message so well, but the story was even more powerful, because later in life that child had to give forgiveness to someone else. That forgiveness came in the form of a peanut butter message. At this point the crowd was a mess, the women could be heard boo-hooing and the men were all choked up.

Your main points need to be enough of a trigger to jar memories and ensure you can expound on the point. Work hard to make your points descriptive so they fully evoke your memory. Consider this:

Good is sometimes great.

This point, at first blush, looks like a great point. However, if you aren't careful, it can be hard to determine context and fail to evoke enough recall to make a solid point. Let's look at this point with a little more description:

As a leader, sometimes good is good enough for the moment.

This will give you far more recall on top of an energetic statement that will draw your listener in. In some cases, your listener will disagree with you and you will have to provide evidence to back up your premise. In other cases, the listener couldn't agree more, and they will be interested in your examples as they match them to their own experiences.

Be very deliberate with your points. Any main point can be used verbatim, as written if you so choose. When you are pulling your main points together, think of three points as the optimum number.

The Power of Threes

Three is a magical number. We have often heard this said about the number three, but do you know about the history of its use? Three is the first number that can create a shape—the triangle. In our thinking, we often triangulate. Bridges often use the stability of the triangle in design. Three describes time or journey—past, present, future; beginning, middle, end; birth, life, death. Even as little children, we are surrounded by threes. The ABC's, Three Blind Mice. The list goes on! Our minds are pretty good at keeping three things straight at a time, but the fourth, fifth and sixth things often slip our minds.

It all comes down to the way we humans process information. We have become proficient at pattern recognition by necessity, and three is the smallest number of elements required to create a pattern. This combination of pattern and brevity results in memorable content, and that's why the Power of Threes will make you a more engaging communicator.

How to Extend Your Content Beyond the Three

Remember I mentioned that I taught my children to outline? After they understood the basics, I taught them that sometimes they would have longer papers that would require a more detailed outline, generally, if they had to write a five to ten-page essay. The main points for a ten-page essay may not fit on an index card. Feel free to expand onto a larger sheet of paper as you find necessary.

From a speaking perspective, whether you are going to be with your in-laws for the weekend, doing a keynote, you may want to use the detailed outline which will ensure you have plenty to talk about for 30 minutes or more. Whenever you need to speak for 15 minutes or even 50, you should use the Power of

Three's. This doesn't mean five points, seven points or more are bad; however, your audience may not be able to retain seven points of information. If you are offering your listeners ongoing access to your content, then by all means, give as many points as you deem necessary to communicate your idea.

When speaking–specifically for longer stints–, organize major talking points in threes utilizing acronyms, analogies and/or relatable words that start with the same letter.

Add value to your audience by enabling them to retain as much value-driving information as possible. Acronyms and analogies both help your audience retain the important information from your speech. Often an audience member will meet me after an event and they will repeat key points of my speech to me. Not only did they receive the message, but they are excited to share with me the common knowledge we now share.

When exploring longer content with the focus on the three power points, you may need to create subpoints. Let's continue the example from before, and change it to be more descriptive:

> *Power Point* - We may often think that good is the enemy of great...

> *Subpoint* - ...but often the situation at hand may not require the additional energy needed for great when good is good enough.

We need to explore this subpoint with some tertiary points. How many tertiary points would you imagine make sense? Take a guess. You got it, three. In certain instances, if your time is limited, I would make the case that two tertiary points are fine.

Threes are easy to get your head around, but less than three gives you time to really delve deeper on fewer subtopics. If you use the tricks mentioned earlier to help your audience retain information, you will win the appreciation of your listeners. If they are jotting notes, they will capture the keywords that will trigger their recall later. When developing your points, in this case tertiary points, make sure they hang nicely off your subpoint. In this case, I will use the following point:

Time may be of the essence but the sole pursuit of great may inhibit your ability to meet time commitments.

The time tertiary point uses the overlap of language, the sole pursuit of great, to keep the audience with you and focused.

Let's add another point:

The information required for great may not be accessible.

The information tertiary point also ties in nicely with the subpoint. Having all the right information at your fingertips may not be possible to make the required decision. Instead of making the right call, you make no call at all.

Sometimes we have to go with our gut or even have to rely on another expert's experience. This doesn't always make us feel the best or most comfortable. However, that is the point. If we wait on too much information, we may never decide at all. A good decision is better than no decision at all when a great decision can't be made.

Let's create another tertiary point, this time with a tag-on sentence:

The money required to be great may not be available. Therefore, it is sometimes more fiscally responsible to be good rather than great.

This set fits extremely well with the main point and with the first subpoint. There are very few who have all the resources they need available to make any endeavor they invest in great. For the rest of us, we may have to reduce the specifications of the product we are developing to stay within the budget, we may have to take some of the bells and whistles off the car that we want, having 500 people at our wedding may have to be reduced to 150. Having the money we need to fulfill our fondest expectations would be great but reducing our scope will lead to a good outcome. With that said, living within our means, or within the budget, is a great decision.

In referencing each of these tertiary points, I will ask the audience to remember my friend TIM: Time, Information & Money. The impact of the acronym is now greater because it relays back to the subpoints that we've so carefully curated. Acronyms are mnemonic devices. They help you remember things. They are links or associations to things we want to hold

TIM

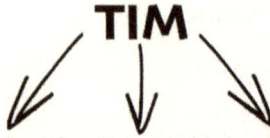

Time may be of the essence, but the sole pursuit of great may inhibit your ability to meet time commitments.

Information required for great may not be accessible.

Money required to be great may not be available. Therefore, it is sometimes more fiscally responsible to be good rather than great.

on to for future use. To be clear, it isn't as much comprehension as it is recall or rote memorization.

While acronyms are not perfect for comprehension, the recall can re-engage your mind where comprehension or further understanding can be gained. As communicators, our objective is to help our listeners derive value out of every word we speak. Consider as you formulate your main points and subpoints how you can leverage acronyms for the benefit of your audience.

With the introduction and the main points out of the way, you can now complete your conclusion. Your conclusion will be two or three sentences, similar to your introduction. The major difference will be the takeaway, or the call-to-action, for the hearers of your message. You can have a quote, a maxim, etc., and you will remind them of the salient points.

There are a few strategic musts when planning your conclusion: Recall, Reflect and Redirect. The most imperative point is that you take the listener back through the introduction and main points. Recall the main ideas of your speech. Reflect on what all of it means to you, and more importantly to your audience. Redirect to a call-to-action after you share your reflection. The takeaway for the audience is the "go get 'em tiger" or the final "umph" that will break the inertia in their lives, so they can be different from when they first entered the auditorium or sat at the table with you.

One approach to closing is to replay the introductory quote or paraphrase it. You could also use another quote if it relates well. Then share the replay of your points with the associated acronym or analogy. Do not rehash the points, merely state them. If you have done a good job you will spark their memory by merely stating your main points. Remember, that the mind retains facts in the Power of Threes. If you want to have a shot at a lasting impression, upgrade your content from a gleeful moment to a lasting memory. I am often shocked when I hear someone say, "One thing you told me that I will never forget," or, "I remember a presentation you gave years ago, and you said something that I remember to this day."

Once you have replayed the central themes, then share the takeaway. You have taken your audience on a journey, and now you must bring them back to the landing strip. They need to be safe, energized and ready for what's next in their lives. Seeing that you have shared this great message with them, what do attendees take away with them? The most precious gift you could give someone is a call-to-action. Anything that will challenge the audience to take the conversation beyond the auditorium or banquet hall or bar. They will know their next steps without any question because you have led them on a journey and gifted them with a clear call-to-action.

After the speech, you may want your audience to receive supplemental materials or take a specific action. Maybe it is driving a different route to work or the encouragement to try something new. The bottom line is you need to give your audience some guidance on what to do with the information you have shared with them. Let's follow this through to its natural conclusion from our example using the topic good being the enemy of great:

> *"I hope you see how good may not be the enemy of great. Especially, when the Time, Information and Money make it impossible to realistically achieve*

greatness. Leo Tolstoy said, 'There is no greatness where there is no simplicity, goodness and truth.' When you find yourself exerting significant energy to attain greatness remember good may be good enough."

You have fully organized your speech and have figured out how to open with an eloquent introduction. You have captured your power points and sanitized them to your meanings and intent as well as defined a thoughtful conclusion. Now it's time to finalize the documentation of this process through your 5x7 cards. The number of cards you use to prepare for a speech will be directly tied to the length of the speech. If one notecard represents one branch, then you will use the same measure to prepare your topic. Now, tuck your cards away in a safe place for immediate or future use.

You can revisit your index cards whenever you have to prepare for a speech or anticipate needing to talk about a topic to someone. Peruse your stack of cards, and based on the audience or event, you can determine which stories you want to tell about yourself that will benefit others. If you are speaking for a specified amount of time, consider how you will distribute your thoughts across the allotted time. I offer a general guideline that is easy to implement. Let's take a 15-minute speech as an example, I would use basic division and distribute time equally from the start: three minutes for your introduction, three minutes for each point, and three minutes for your conclusion. Keep in mind that you can always move things around but focus on a balanced speech.

The main idea of the outline with a few points is that it gives you the flexibility to customize on the go. You may have an interaction with someone from the audience that you can draw into your speech moments before being asked to speak. If you memorize your speech, it becomes very difficult to leverage this technique. The purpose of the outline is to ensure we hone our energy on the connection with the listener.

> If you are going to a social event, grab four or five index cards, and use those in case you get stuck during small talk. Keep the cards in your pocket and sneak a peek if you hit a wall in conversation. Pull them out when you step away to go to the restroom or grab a call, and re-engage ready for the next round of conversation. One hint: it's probably best not to hold the cards in casual settings.

The brief outline of the 5 x 7 cards enables you to have a lot of freedom in your delivery. Remember, the best use of the notecard is to have your introduction, three points (remembering The Power of Threes), and your conclusion. Don't overdo it and keep it simple for effective communication.

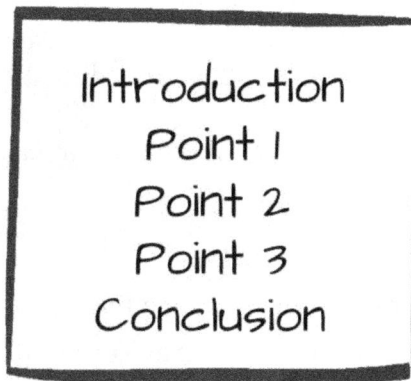

```
Introduction
  Point 1
  Point 2
  Point 3
 Conclusion
```

Chapter 3

Tailor & Accessorize Your Message

"You can't have style if you don't have substance."
- *Ozwald Boateng*

I remember the first time I bought a great suit. The fabric was amazing, and it looked just perfect in the shop. It looked like a suit that would make me stand taller and speak louder. I knew this was the suit that would bring me a winning proposal on the next project and a promotion. I got the suit home and realized I had spent so much time looking at the color and the details of the suit that I had neglected to spend a lot of time considering the fit.

The suit looked great on the hanger, but it didn't fit me like I had envisioned. The pants needed to be hemmed, and the beautiful fabric of the jacket's arms extended well past a fashionable length at the wrists. I had purchased a great suit, but my work was just beginning. I saw the suit fitting well in my mind, but the way I saw the suit in my mind's eye did not match with the present reality. Sometimes, when your vision doesn't line up with truth you can feel disappointed. However, in the case of the new suit, there was a solution. Taking my suit to a tailor who could make the suit match the picture in my mind would bring my vision to reality.

Preparing a speech is a lot like finding the right suit. You need the right basics before you can elevate to the next level. You may have the fit, but it could be a bit tight in the waist, or the jacket might be snug across the chest. This is when you focus on tailoring—providing a custom fit. A professional takes your measurements to refine the fit to bring in or let out certain areas.

When the tailor returns the suit to you, it fits perfectly. As time goes on, you may need additional adjustments, but the suit is customized to you. It won't fit anyone else like it fits you. The subtlety in this analogy to conversation and speaking is you are fitting a message around your listeners as you fit a suit around yourself.

Your topic can be like good-fitting work attire. You can start with one off the rack, but you will want to add some tailoring to make it attractive to your listeners. In some instances, a little touch here or there will work. Other times, more dramatic personalization is needed. Take the time to customize your message to the specific audience. A canned message that has been delivered, rehearsed and delivered again in the exact same way will lack emotion and leave your audience feeling like they missed something.

Once I was asked to give a talk about motivation and goals. The catch was I only had five minutes. The speech I usually give is about 15-20 minutes. There was no way to speak fast enough to get all my content into a five-minute spiel. Moreover, a simple removal of a section wouldn't suffice because of the way the points built upon each other. I would need to cut each section and retool my main points in order to boil them down to their purest essence. I was pleasantly surprised at the result of my strategic cuts. The audience connected with the material and didn't feel cheated one bit on the length.

I believe that being a good conversationalist, whether impromptu or scheduled, is achievable if you are cognizant of your content and tasteful in your tailoring. William Shakespeare said, "Conversation should be pleasant without scurrility, witty without affection, free without indecency, learned without conceitedness, novel without falsehood." I think what Mr. Shakespeare was getting at is the importance of balance in any conversation.

The equilibrium in the tone of your words by being pleasant without vulgarity (scurrility), witty without too many inside jokes, transparent without sharing irrelevant information, knowledgeable without appearing arrogant, and sharing new material without relying on lies to further your message. This level of mindfulness really considers the person you are communicating with and makes conversing and listening to you pleasurable. With the recipe of all these ingredients, you have crafted a well-tailored message.

Bring the most current material and the best you have to offer each time you present.

The decision to tailor a message can seem daunting because you worry about the extra time it will take to prepare. Have no fear! You can create an engaging presentation with some simple tips that you can apply to any topic. Your listeners will appreciate the extra effort and will think you spent hours more preparing, when in fact your polished presentation is a result of careful planning and customizing.

Basic Tailoring

One of the most powerful lessons I have learned is people love to hear their name. Dale Carnegie in his book, *How to Win Friends and Influence People*, states that they're the most powerful words that people love to hear. Whether you are talking one-on-one or addressing a larger group, people want to feel that you identify with them on an individual level. They want to feel seen and heard. Carnegie said it best, "You can make more friends in two months by becoming interested in other people than you can in two years by trying to get other people interested in you."

Think about the last time you went to a concert. That group was probably touring months before they reached you, and they most likely started the concert the same way in every city they played, *"Hello [insert city name]!"* The crowd always roars in approval because they have been personally acknowledged and feel seen by the band. This example of simple tailoring is subtle and effective.

Simple tailoring adds to the edges of your speech and doesn't change the shape of the core message.

The audience won't tweet about the "Hello Chicago." They may, however, share how the concert made them feel connected to the performer. A good show will include the band reacting to the audience, playing louder when people are cheering, and adding an extra solo to keep the crowd on their feet. In the same way, a great speaker will gauge reaction and share the message with a nod toward the people listening.

Whenever I am out and about, and I overhear someone say Chicago, I immediately perk up and look over in the direction of that conversation. The word "Chicago" piques my interest because that's where I'm from and, therefore, have had a myriad of experiences there. I personally identify with Chicago so it's like they are talking about me. Word cues like cities and group names can work to capture the interest of your listeners.

An easy way to engage the audience is to identify some of the larger groups of people present at that event. If you can speak to the audience and call out those groups, you will be able to add specificity as you go, and they will feel you are speaking to them directly.

The audience will feel that your message was written precisely for them, and in a way, it was.

Let's say you are in Philadelphia. If you take the stage and say, "Philly, how's everyone doing?" I guarantee you will get a response—and a positive one at that. Follow that up with, *I heard this is the city of brotherly love...is that true?* Even more applause and engagement. *"Well I see the Fire Department's in the house."* Target the largest group in the room and give them a mention from your platform. Your crowd may become so amped up that you might have to settle them down. When you get the crowd excited, you want to make sure you can match the intensity that you have created with your message. There is nothing worse than getting the crowd hyped and failing to deliver an equally compelling message.

Advanced Tailoring

Advanced tailoring cuts to the very core of your message. You can truly customize your content for a high-level impact to the audience. Your examples should be recognizable to the audience and show that you took time to research and prepare for the event. The best way to illustrate this concept is to convert your professional examples to examples from another industry. Let's take a look at the legal and health industries:

If you are a doctor presenting to a group of doctors, you will use the language you typically use at the office. You may mention the latest technology or laugh about the hang-ups you encounter every day with patients. Presenting to an audience of your peers has its own challenges but tailoring a speech to appeal to them particularly is usually simple. You are, in essence, presenting to yourself as the target market. You already know where you're coming from and what you are talking about.

Now, let's say you are a doctor presenting to a group of lawyers. You could talk about the latest technology and how it's helping your patients. You could share a funny story about the oddities at the office. The key difference between speaking in front of your peers versus speaking in front of other industries is in how the speech is built, tailored and delivered.

You aren't just hemming the pants; you are re-cutting the fabric to make a new garment—in this case, a new conversation altogether. Think about it this way, lawyers think about different challenges than doctors. Their humor is probably different given their individual career paths. I remember joining a technology team and trying to communicate humor in one of my examples. Being primarily a numbers and process person, I found my jokes were often met with blank stares. If they told each other a joke they would be laughing hysterically, and I would be on the periphery wondering what was so funny.

> The key difference between speaking in front of your peers vs. speaking in front of other industries is how the speech is delivered, built and tailored.

Chapter 3: Tailor & Accessorize Your Message

Don't assume all content is universal. It may need to be tailored to fit the situation and the group of listeners. There is a more serious side to tailoring. Nothing fails more than untimely commentary in the wake of sensitive issues that may be impacting a person in your audience. Celebrating the birth of a new baby in the presence of someone who recently experienced a miscarriage can create a painful, and awkward, moment. The joy of new life should always be celebrated, but the key is sensitivity to the feelings of those around you.

I remember an incident from some time ago; I was having a wonderful conversation with a colleague, and we arrived on the topic of their recently deceased parent. My response was, "Well, we all have to go that way." The conversation ended abruptly, and I sensed some awkwardness. I mentioned the conversation to a few folks, and they said I was rude and completely insensitive to make that comment.

In my mind, I was just conveying sentiments I had heard from a recent family member in helping me deal with the loss of my mom. I guess I should have figured out that it wasn't a universal or appropriate comment for anyone's passing. In the context it was shared with me, the phrase was delivered by a close friend known for their direct language. Lesson learned? Be careful to consider the emotional implication of your communications. Everything isn't funny to everyone all the time. Tailoring could keep a valued and trusted relationship intact.

Time to Accessorize

Now that you have tailored the suit for the occasion, let's have some fun and accessorize your speech. When you purchase a garment, you may need a new tie, belt, necklace or a handkerchief to bring it together. Or you may want to add a bracelet or a ring to dress it up. A great tailor, stylist and haberdasher are experts of putting those special touches on your look. These additions do not change the outfit in any permanent way, but they bring it to life with the right accessories. There are four types of accessories that can breathe new life into an existing speech or make the speech more provocative:

1. Words
2. Quotes
3. Language
4. Emphasis

Accessorize with Words

Word choice can help to stimulate or disengage the minds of your audience. Poor word choice can throw off the audience and make them wonder what you're talking about. Folks in the audience might not realize right away, but subconsciously many instantly think, *I don't think that is the right word. Is that the right word? What is that word? I'm not familiar.* If they get stuck here, they can tune out and lose important pieces of your message.

Also, realize that the words you use can backfire. If you choose a word that doesn't resonate with the audience, some will write it off, and keep listening. Others will become mentally paralytic, ruminating on the definition of the words you have used. Most inquisitive folks will try to figure out what you are trying to say and will utterly stop following your message until they get an answer. The point of accessorizing with words is more about clever word substitutions that will appeal to the ears. As speakers, you must recognize that you have all types of people in the audience: people who want to be there, people who don't want to be there, people who like to be entertained, and everyone in between.

In an excerpt from one of my speeches, I talk about Newton's Second Law of Motion. I could say the phrase, "Because it's an equation, it doesn't apply to my speech today." The statement is clear, yet it is very dry and boring, and it begs the question: *why bring it up in the first place?* My delivery in practice is this: "Newton's Second Law of Motion is F=MxA. I am not going to spend time here because, given the time, I would not be able to eloquently articulate the essence of said equation." If I have a great connection with the audience, I let them in on my excursion by saying, "That's just a fancy way of saying I've learned to stay away from equations." Generally, it's worth a laugh, and at the very least, it is entertaining.

Your best friend, as you accessorize with words, is the age-old thesaurus. You can find unlimited substitutions with equivalent meaning for most words. The 'technical' term is synonyms. However, I like to use the word substitution because in practice I typically write a word and look to substitute it with another word—a synonym. I picked this up from my experience as a musician. In music, we often talk about chord substitutions or inversions, which is an equivalent replacement chord or synonym.

These days, one needs only take a moment to visit Thesaurus.com, type a word to search for synonyms, and voila! Countless substitutions! To reinforce my point, caution on the side of conservatism when selecting your substitutions. Make sure your substitutes are words you can pronounce and are confident your audience will be able to comprehend.

How I like to employ accessorizing with words is to practice my speech, write a detailed outline, and sprinkle simple but decorative substitutions such as:

- Journey to Excursion
- Alive to Animated
- Difficult to Challenging
- Profitable to Lucrative
- Happy to Felicitous
- Excited to Elated

The key to elevating your language is to internalize the emotions that words bring in the context of the speech. If I am telling a mischievous story about one of my kids, and I share that they are going through a 'difficult phase,' most parents would know what I meant. Nonetheless, adding the descriptor of "troublesome" to the story brings a more seasoned aspect to the story. The perfect words can set the atmosphere and provide greater context, enabling an alternative tone or evoking an emotional response from your listeners.

Words that are overused can leave your message taken for granted. Take care to be aggressive about word substitution but be cautious in deployment. Ensure your words are easily deciphered within the context of the story you are sharing.

Now that you're equipped with the words that you need, let's make sure that people can understand what you say. You have probably heard the words enunciation and articulation. Speaking clearly so that your audience understands every word is vital. Misunderstandings lead to inaccurate perceptions that create uncomfortable moments. The real tragedy is that the speaker doesn't know that they have been misunderstood.

If you want to improve your enunciation, practice tongue twisters. One tip on tongue twisters is to work on the verbal hiccups you struggle with. For example, if s's are your hang up, practice: "She sells seashells by the seashore." If p's trip up your tongue, try "Peter Piper picked a peck of pickled peppers." Tongue twisters are not just for kids, they are used by many professions to increase smooth communication from acting to public speaking.

Accessorize with Quotes

As stated before, open your speech with an impactful quote from someone you respect. You don't have to stick with the traditional quotes, quotes from leaders who passed on hundreds of years ago, or even quotes from people who are only well-known. Share a quote from an expert on the topic you are presenting, or a quote that is meaningful to the story you are telling.

Audience members are seeking phrases that will stay with them. Use short quotations and add your own insight to them. It's well and good to share your favorite quote but add some personal history to connect it with your message. Some great places to find quotes may be as close as your nightstand. What books are you reading? What conversations have you had that you could quote to your listeners? Just like you can accessorize with word choice, relevant quotes are no more than a Google search away. When reading, I like to take a notecard and jot down key phrases to utilize later. You can adapt this practice for your own purposes by keeping your ears open when you hear a fellow speaker or are watching a movie.

One of my favorite quotes from the Star Wars movie, *The Empire Strikes Back,* is when Luke Skywalker is in Jedi training with Yoda attempting to levitate Skywalker's fallen ship. Yoda tells him to use the force. In frustration, Luke shrugs, "Alright, I'll give it a try." Yoda sternly returns, "No! Try not. Do or do not. There is no try." Yoda's words have been repeated by movie-goers since that movie's release in 1980.

Write down the quotes that you can't stop thinking about. It could be the advice given by Yoda in Star Wars or something your mother always said to you growing up. Chances are that the quotes that resonate with you will also resonate in the minds of your listeners. You can also take that handy 5x7 card and use it as a bookmark to write down quotes and thoughts as you read through a book or daily reading. Quotes sometimes say what you wanted to say more effectively. However, don't feel as if you need to rely on sayings or quotes. Remember, *you* are connecting with someone. Only use quotes that consist in conveying your message and *always* give credit where credit is due.

One other consideration should be mentioned. Quotes may move you, but they may not move your audience. If there is a particular emotion that is evoked by the quote, it's your job to evoke that emotion in your listeners.

Accessorize with Language

The one thing that ignites me more than words and quotes is the use of powerful language. We have so many tools in language to express our ideas. As a conversationalist, it is in your best interest to become familiar with these tools. You will be stronger in some than others, and at least having a working knowledge of all, along with the mastery of a few, will unleash a joy for communicating.

The good news is I'm not going to take you on a long English lesson, but I am going to give you a list of the language tools and mechanisms that will unlock new opportunities for how you communicate:

- **Anecdote** – a brief witty story. Anecdotes create audience-to-message connections and strengthen recall because people remember stories.

- **Aphorism** – expression of belief; a proverb often lending credence to your message. It can be associated with quotes.

- **Alliteration** – repeating consonants or syllables in a phrase. This can heighten the memorization of the speaker and audience.

- **Allegory** – a message using strong symbolism for real-world occurrences. It strengthens your points for recall and maximum impact.

- **Homonym** – a word pronounced the same as another but differing in meaning. (You can have a lot of fun with this technique. I have used the phrase the 'son's raise' as a substitute for the 'sun's rays.' Most effective in written communication. When used effectively, this can be thought-provoking by your audience.

- **Homily** – a lesson or lecture, often spiritual in nature. This technique can be a great tool for religious audiences.

- **Idiom** – an expression or saying that is not the traditional definition of the words used. It is great for crowds that speak your native language or the language that you are speaking. Idioms are not great for foreign audiences.

- **Metaphor** – a figure of speech or comparison of things that have a quality in common. Less obvious than a simile.

- **Simile** – a figure of speech comparing things in a direct way, using like or as. Less nuanced than a metaphor.

- **Triad** – a set of three loosely connected ideas; this is the literary version of the Power of Three.

Grasping these literary concepts and using them skillfully has made me a better communicator. The more you use these when verbalizing your ideas, the better you become at applying these tools.

Accessorize with Emphasis

Several years ago, I heard an example that notified me of the importance of emphasis. Where emphasis is placed in a sentence can change its entire meaning. This is one of the reasons I don't like email and texting as a primary communication vehicle. Have you received a text and misunderstood the meaning? It confused you, made you anxious, or sent you off in a panic. You later find that your unease was unmerited and led to an unnecessary, and perhaps even unfortunate, overreaction.

Consider the following sentence: "I didn't say he ate the apple." At first glance, this innocuous statement seems very straightforward, *I didn't say he ate the apple.* Change the emphasis to a distinct word and see how the intonation (and interpretation) of the sentence changes.

Example A

I didn't say he ate the apple.

Example B

I didn't say he ate the apple.

Example C

I didn't say he ate the apple.

In Example A, he may have eaten the apple, but I am not stating that I know that. It could imply someone else knows that he ate the apple. In Example B, the man may not be the person who ate the apple. I am not sure. It could have been him or a third party yet to be identified. In Example C, he ate something, but it may not have been the apple.

In this simple sentence with a pronoun and some fruit, there is a lot of room for ambiguity. Emphasis should be applied in an intentional way when you are communicating to your listeners.

Experiment with this concept in your own communication. You will hear the difference and train your ear to place emphasis in key areas that you want to stress in your messages.

Another way to emphasize your points is to use repetition. When you want to remind your listeners of ideas, words, and phrases, imagery is effective. Repetition, however, is only effective when not over-done.

Which Suit to Wear?

Another important part of connecting with your audience is the positioning of your message. Will it be highly relatable and enable the audience to be with you in the story? Or will you be appealing to their intellect, challenging listeners with high-level vocabulary and unexplored philosophies? In the same way, there are outfits for different occasions, there are topics and types of content for unique situations. A wedding might require a tux, evening gown or very formal attire; whereas a picnic may require something more casual like a t-shirt and jeans.

Cerebral messages work best when you are dealing with technical audiences or how-to sessions.

Otherwise, lean towards being tangible—aka relatable. This does not mean you can't appeal to the intellect of your audience or teach your listeners new things. I love putting my knowledge of skyscrapers in my speeches, but I think we can all agree no matter how it's built, who contracted the land or what's inside the building, we all get queasy when looking down—whether you're afraid of heights or not. Being highly formal and extemporaneous when uncalled for will make you seem pretentious and prideful, and as if you are trying to display your expertise through showing off how much you know.

An audience is more interested in what value you deliver versus how much impressive vernacular you can string together. There is a dissimilarity between being yourself and being what you think the audience wants you to be. Trying to impress people frequently leaves you with egg on your face. This is where mentoring and feedback can help. Someone who can tell you they found your speech was a bit verbose for the audience can help you improve your future engagements. They can watch the audience response and let you know how they thought it went. A mentor can tell you about any subconscious behavior they observed. This feedback will help you develop into your best version of your conversationalist self.

Chapter 4

Use the Power of Storytelling

"What I was interested in was conveying an emotional message, which means using everything you've got inside you sometimes to barely make a note, or if you have to strain to sing, you sing."

- *Nina Simone*

Which do you prefer: going to a meeting or going to a movie? Unless you really love meetings more than a night out, chances are you would rather go to the movies. Meetings are infamous for being boring and often pointless. A movie has an opening that grabs you, a plot that captures your imagination. Well, at least a really good one!

As a speaker on any topic, you can influence your listeners best through great storytelling. Whether you must give directives, inspire or inform, you can employ storytelling for added effect. There are stories that are terrible and won't advance your message, but often those stories don't follow the guidelines below:

- **A story must be relatable.** The setting, the characters, the central theme—they all need to be pivotal to the audience, or the story will fall flat, and they may as well have attended a meeting.

- **A good story has a plot and setting.** A plot consists of a beginning, middle and end. The key is detail without being lengthy and ensuring the audience can visualize the setting. One aspect in many a story is the location of the story. To say a house in the country is good, but to say a small cottage on the outer edge of the Adirondacks in Upstate New York is far better. Include the colors, the season, or time of year. The audience will be able to picture themselves in the setting. Some may even be able to hear the surrounding environment or smell the air because they have visited the very place that you describe.

- **A great story has vivid imagery.** The characters are more than a mother or father, son or a daughter. They have height and weight; colored and textured hair; vibrant eyes of blue, brown or green. The people in the story you share have attitudes and dispositions. Describing the characters in this way will make them seem more real and help the members of the audience visualize themselves within the scene(s) of the story.

Once your story meets the three guidelines above, you are ready to further develop the story. This story can be fact or fiction. There is no need to differentiate in front of an audience. If the story serves your purpose, let the crowd decide whether to believe all the facets of the story or not. After the foundation is established, you will want to bring in moments of drama. Even happy stories have moments of conflict, and there are many tried and true narrative arcs. It could be the good guy, bad guy plot. It could be overcoming natural disasters or social ills that we all worry about, e.g. tornadoes, viruses, animal cruelty, AIDS, etc.

As you craft the story, the drama you lace throughout your story should pull your audience in. If you are against hunting, the best time to address your anti-animal cruelty belief may not be in front of a bunch of weekend hunters. You may not realize it until the end of your speech, but there will be snarling throughout the crowd, furrowed brows and crossed arms. If you do begin a story with a clear conflict in mind, be mindful of how you present the other side. Sharing your viewpoint with equal compassion and conviction to the "other side" can be powerful and thought-provoking. The conflict and subsequent tension that ensues in a story is the torque that will send your story soaring.

Consider when you watch any movie and are gripped by the conflict, the anticipation of how it will turn out. Often, you are more interested by what you didn't expect or a strange twist than the actual explosion or car chase. As you are building your tension, add unexpected surprises and shocking twists to keep the audience interested. When I watch a "who done it" movie with my family, we are so certain it's the butler, and it turns out to be the quarrelsome neighbor. We are fascinated to understand how we missed it.

Once the conflict reaches a climax, there must be a resolution. Good or bad, there needs to be a culmination of all the backstory you shared with the audience. As Anton Chekov, the Russian playwright and master of the modern short story, wrote, *if you say in the first chapter that there is a rifle hanging on the wall, by the second or third chapter, it absolutely must go off.* Resolution is what we all crave because it attaches the hope of a solution and provides a sense of relief. That hope could be for the future of all, or if the resolution is less than favorable, you can attach it to the need for further commitment for a brighter tomorrow.

Storytelling comes easy to some and can be extremely difficult for others, but whatever camp you find yourself in, know where you are on the spectrum. No point illustrates this more than a story I once heard that I have adapted over the years.

The Marching 100[3] took to the field but once a year. The best musicians from marching bands around the country came together in a small

---

[3] The Marching 100 is Florida A&M University's marching band that has been credited for not less than 30 innovative techniques which have become standard operating procedures for many high school and collegiate marching band programs throughout the nation.

town just north of Rockford, IL. Each year at the beginning of the football season, the Marching 100 would take the field to put on the greatest musical performance of the year.

One year on a bright, September day, the sun shone bright. The wind was still. The Marching 100 took the field as they have for decades. As usual, their formations were flawless; their musicianship was fantastic. However, unlike always, on one formation 99 of the marching 100 went left and one of the Marching 100 went right. The crowd gasped, nothing like this had ever happened. Just as quickly as the incident caught the crowd's attention the Marching 100 were joined again and completed a spectacular show.

Afterwards the Bandmaster asked the one Marching 100 band member what happened out there. The band member thought for a moment and said, "Sir, I am not sure what caused 99 of our marching brigades to go the wrong way." The bandmaster asked if it could have been him that went the wrong way. The band member said, "No I have thought about it and I am sure I made the right turn. I'm not sure what went wrong with everyone else."

You and your audience are one—make sure that you are all on the same page. You could very well find yourself saying I don't understand why those 99 people in the audience just don't get it.

Connecting with the Physical

Communication always begins with nonverbal cues. As a parent, I've learned how important this is when interacting with my children. I note when I give an instruction whether they cross their arms and fold their brow or walk away without making eye contact. Conversely, it's much more pleasant when they are happy and smiling when I come home. My favorite is when they do something great, and I beam with pride. I will look over, and they are showing the same proud grin on their faces that I wear on mine. Consider the workplace. You will find non-verbal cues from your boss when he is not happy that you are late, points his finger to his watch, and gives you that stern brow that your 4-year old just gave you that morning. Contrarily, the warm handshake from a colleague indicates that they respect you and are glad to be working with you.

The physicality of communicating cannot be ignored or underestimated. The ability of a story to come to life or the power to strongly convey a point can be effectively emphasized with appropriate gestures. I want to strongly suggest that the physicality of communicating with body language is a technique and not only a natural inclination. We all know people who are very expressive. They are known for talking with their hands and for their exaggerated facial expressions. When they communicate, they naturally draw people into their story. They captivate, motivate and influence whomever they come into contact with.

The first step to building great gestures is a prepared communication. With a prepared oration, you have the opportunity to craft in, append or inject very specific gestures at key points of your message for maximum impact. Below is a list of key places to insert your gestures:

- **Statements on Directions:** up or down, east or west, left or right, etc.
- **Moods:** happy, sad, angry, confused, etc.
- **Size:** big, small, tall, short, et

- **Activities:** counting money, lifting, hammering, etc.

You can develop the technique of gesturing by preparing before your speeches. Develop a set of reliable gestures that you can rely on through recall and muscle memory. These added abilities will also be at your beck-and-call for impromptu speaking and conversations. Make sure you are far enough along in mastering these gestures before you start employing them in a live setting. Better to be stiff and effective, and even considered *too* formal, than to be fidgety and misunderstood.

The biggest mistake any speaker can make is communicating one thing and the audience hearing something different.

Incorporating gestures should strengthen your communication, not confuse or confound. If you say up and point down, you create a disconnect that must be reconciled. Hopefully you catch it in the moment and get your audience back on the right track. Often, we assume that the members of the audience get our point. *"Oh, they know what I meant."* Never assume listeners understand. Some people are purists, meaning they will take what you say at face value. In one-on-one conversations, you can explain yourself. In larger audiences, they won't necessarily get the same clarifications.

It is important to be intentional with your gestures. Recognize the impact if you incorrectly gesture to describe someone's size and make the gesture for a large and round person. You're negatively impacting someone's self-image. With that in mind, when you are not intentionally gesturing, keep your hands and body quiet. Relaxed hands at your side with a pleasant gaze is best for creating a neutral posture. Clasping your hands or folding your arms may communicate nervousness. If you naturally move your hands often, this will require practice. Have someone watch and give you feedback to find out if you are moving needlessly.

Gestures like leaning toward someone slightly while not invading their space demonstrates that you are keenly interested in what they are saying. You are giving them your full, undivided attention. Try this the next time you are at a happy hour with co-workers or eating dinner with your family. Look in their eyes and lean in toward them. Note what you notice from them.

As you read through the outline of your speech, ponder all the places where gestures can be worked in and jot them down. Then, practice the gestures. Some will feel awkward at first, but you will get better at it, more natural. Find those gestures that don't work and remove them from the repertoire. Again, better to be stiff and effective than fidgety and misunderstood.

I leave this section with the most powerful gesture of all. Can you guess what it is? It can light up a room. It can make a sad person feel better. It has healing powers. "When you're smiling, the whole world smiles with you." Smile at someone, and that person will often smile back. A warm, genuine smile works magic in communications. Nodding your head affirmatively as you look at someone in the audience works in concert with a smile. Commit to the triple threat, a smile, a nod, and a yes, and the magic is immeasurable.

Another discipline you will need to master is managing non-essential movement. On occasion, you will encounter orators who pace when they speak. This movement can make the audience feel like they are at a tennis match, or worse, make the audience as nervous as the speaker appears to be. It is imperative to only move when needed to avoid unnecessary distractions. You don't want your message to get misconstrued.

This leads us to a concept known as "staging." Staging allows you to use designated areas of the stage to help your story unfold as well as assist your listeners with recall. If you were to talk about your life in three stages, you could use the right side of the stage for your childhood, the center for your adolescence, and finally the left as your adulthood. I have done this right-to-left (which will be left-to-right for your audience). This is the way we read, so it helps flow the story in the mind of your audience. A neat way to do this in one-on-one conversation or a small group is to use purposeful hand gestures. You can establish a setting on the right, center and left sides of your body.

Here is what I have learned about movement when speaking to a larger audience and a stage is involved: stand center stage, as applicable, hands rested at side and begin making good eye contact with those in front of you. Gradually move to one side of the room and return to the rested position. Make eye contact with those in that vicinity; move to the other side via a stop center stage and finish center stage.

The important point is that you are creating anchors for your message by using staging. Every area of the stage means something; it correlates to your message. Each time you are at a specific point of the stage, the audience should recall the location and the correlation.

You will find practicing your gestures, staging in front of mirrors, or video recording yourself will help your communication immensely. Watching yourself will give you great feedback and allow you to make necessary adjustments. The physical aspects of speaking are critical to conveying strong messages, effectively engaging your audience and succeeding in speaking.

Chapter 5

Connect with Your Audience

"Making the simple complicated is commonplace; making the complicated simple, awesomely simple, that's creativity."

- *Charles Mingus*

Connecting with your family, peers, constituents and others is one of the most important tasks a communicator is tasked with. In conversation or giving a speech, you want to add value to the lives you are engaged with. If you can't connect, you can't add value. I remember one of my first speaking engagements at a church. I had developed a speech on weight loss: the joys of healthy eating and how it is a spiritual principle. I didn't do any homework on the members of the church, who all came from the generation where the way to anyone's heart is through their stomach. They also didn't appreciate my liveliness. Being a more conservative crowd, I must have looked like Elvis gyrating on the *Ed Sullivan Show*. I wasn't asked back. Perhaps the content was great, but I did not connect to the audience on any level.

If you cannot connect with the audience, then they cannot download the information. It's like trying to connect with a server to download text or an image on your computer—if you don't have a connection, you cannot get the information. Sometimes, you can start with a solid connection, but the connection becomes corrupted. You lose your information that you were trying to download, and we all know how frustrating that can be. Plus, it can be difficult to get back online once the connection is lost. It is the same in communicating: once you lose the listener, you will struggle to get reconnected. Be cognizant of the disconnect you can create for your listeners. If not resolved, these disconnects can re-shape how people view you, your message, and their understanding of your message. I heard a comedian say the first time you are meeting your audience, it is a one-to-many conversation. After your audience has followed you for a time, those that are supporters continue the journey, and others fall away, the conversation becomes one-to-one. The group has understood who you are and decided to stay engaged. If you mis-step and miscommunicate, you can lose the audience's support. We have heard of leaders losing their followers because they did, said or expressed support for something their followers didn't associate with their character.

Great content is invaluable and a must for building your reputation as a communicator, but if you cannot connect with the audience, your impeccable content will fall on deaf ears. There is nothing more unsettling than standing in front of a crowd, and you don't sense a connection. The connection gives you confidence; it allows you to give your best because you feel safe and unencumbered. If you have any inclination that you are boring your listeners, you will only reinforce your feelings of insecurity. The blank stares and empty eyes can drain your confidence, a portent of imminent disaster. When I am listening to a speaker and there isn't a connection, though I may try and press on, sometimes I get drowsy and my mind wanders. The worst thing to see from the stage is a sleepy audience! I want to give you the tools to make and *keep* a connection throughout your presentation.

How to Start Investigating Your Audience

In most situations, we know who is in our audience. We have preparation time, we have information on preferred themes and intentions for the event, as well as expected outcomes from the organizers. All of this information can help us make the right choices in tailoring great communications. However, on occasion you may be asked to fill-in for someone. The keynote has come down with a bug or is delayed and can't make it. When filling in last minute, you may not know who the members of the audience are: How do you connect? Whether you are well informed or going into your speaking opportunity blind, you can use the following steps to help you connect with members of your audience. The most important elements of connecting with your audience is truly knowing their purpose and tailoring and accessorizing your message accordingly.

Knowing your audience begins with a short investigation. Often, we are afraid to ask too many questions. James Nathan Miller offers the best advice:

"There is no such thing as a worthless conversation, provided you know what to listen for. And questions are the breath of life for a conversation." We have a general sense of things, and we go with it. To truly get to know your audience, you need to become a sleuth of sorts. Ask questions, and don't be afraid to aggressively pursue answers about your incoming listeners. You can ask the meeting planner or contact about the people in the audience during the planning stages of the event.

Questions to ask:

- Who are the sponsors of this event?
- What does a successful event look like?
- Did audience members pay to attend?
- What do the audience members hope to learn today?
- What are the hopes and expected outcomes of the organizers of this event?
- Who are the people that will be joining us today?
- What are their affiliations?
- Are they connected to one another through friends, family or an organization?

- Does the group have diverse backgrounds, or are they aligned on professional or social affiliations?

Some of the questions above can also be answered through a quick informal chat with attendees the day of the event. The key is to realize that you are the listener during this exercise and disproportionately listening over speaking. Lou Holz famously said, "I never learn anything talking. I only learn things when I ask questions." You may have noticed a speaker arrive a full day before they are scheduled to present. They are sitting among the guests, and if you watch them, they will be intently listening, learning about the people and the organization. In Chapter 3 I discussed weaving in content specific to your audience. A speaker who actively integrates themselves is able to do this effectively.

Open-ended questions avoid the yes and no answers or short response.

One note on investigation probing: all questions should be open-ended questions. This will allow your subject the opportunity to give you numerous inputs to work with. Open-ended questions avoid the yes-or-no answer or short response. If I ask, *"Is it hot outside?"* I have narrowed the possible responses down to yes or no. If I adjust slightly to ask, *"How is the weather outside?"* I give the responder the opportunity to give a fuller, more creative answer. Assuredly, some of this is just the personality of the responder. Give your responder room to give you as much information as possible so you can tailor your message to the audience which drives a great connection.

Once your investigation is nearly complete, take the next step and dig deeper. Interrogation is often considered negatively. When the police bring someone in for questioning, they take them into the interrogation room to ask sharp questions that may make the suspect uncomfortable. However, the literal definition of interrogate suggests that we are seeking answers to questions that the suspect may deem somewhat personal or private. We are looking for more complex answers than the investigation may have revealed. From your own investigating, if you have your antennae up, you will notice that several of the folks you questioned may have more to say or more input that will make your speech that much more successful.

If you envision an interrogation from a movie — or an unfortunate circumstance that landed you in the interrogation room—you notice a difference in the questions. They are not open-ended. *Did you do this? Was this your motive?* Most interrogators are very direct, looking for the yes or no, short answers. This is because the majority of the information to close the case has been collected. Now, we want the final confession that will bring this case to a close. You may find out that half the crowd are die hard L.A. Lakers fans and the other half Boston Celtics fans. Knowing the heat behind this rivalry, you may want to choose your tailoring very carefully. You may want to ask is the crowd friendly despite the difference in team preference. A *no* means steer clear; it's not worth the risk of alienating half of your listeners. A *yes* would suggest you could really add an effective element to your speech. *How many Lakers fans out there? That's pretty good, but I heard there were some Celtics fans out there too. How are my Celtics fans doing?* You will have the crowd stoked.

The way to look at it is investigate many, interrogate few. You will spend more time with someone in interrogation versus investigation. Your investigative questions may be 30-60 seconds each. That means the two to three folks you consider interrogating would be finished within one to three minutes. You'll be surprised how much information you are able to glean from someone in that time. Plus, if you find a person that is passionate about the event you are speaking at and wants you to succeed, hang onto your hat because you will get far more insight than you bargained for.

This idea allows you to learn and speak the language of your listeners. I believe this is one of the most important things you can do to drive a powerful bond with your listeners. You will be able to tailor your message to that audience with a snug-fitting speech. This feels like a bit of overkill for a dinner date. Understand that all these principles work in big or small interactions and doses. You may need to make an appropriate adjustment. Maybe you are called last minute to have dinner with the in-laws or on a spur of the moment date. Let's look at several questions that work in preparation for taking someone out on a date or any other casual one-on-one encounter. You can search on the internet for some information, but no stalking please. Keep it classy.

Questions to ask:

- What is his/her favorite type of food?
- What are his/her interests such as movies or sports? Why is this an interest?

- Any brothers and sisters? Weird uncles? Favorite cousins?
- What line of work are they in?
- Any pets?

Gathering this information will help you speak his or her language. Don't try to use it to impress or to play gotcha. You are after the connection. Your desire is to speak the same language, to tailor your conversation appropriately. Being an insightful, caring and thought-provoking conversationalist will make you and your comrade's evening memorable at the very least and at the most very enjoyable.

Music is the Answer

One of my favorite songs from my teen years was *Music is the Answer* by Colonel Abrams. It describes music as the remedy for many of our social ills. Nothing can bring people together like music. Music crosses so many pre-drawn cultural lines. Consider the tenets of music to connect with your listeners. You can reel your audience in using music as the answer.

In the previous chapter, I talked about the power of words. When you consider the lyrics in a song, they can be powerful in connecting your message. What would happen if you added these musical quotes to a speech:

"I can't get no, satisfaction"
– *Satisfaction* by The Rolling Stones

"Some will win, some will lose.
Some were born to sing the blues.
Oh, the movie never ends.
It goes on and on and on and on"
 – *Don't Stop Believin'* by Journey

"Even the genius asks questions."
– *Me Against the World* by Tupac

"If we weren't all crazy, we would go insane."
– *Changes in Latitude, Changes in Attitudes* by Jimmy Buffett

"An honest man's pillow is his peace of mind."
– *Minutes to Memories* by John Cougar Mellencamp

"Don't ask me what I think of you,
I might not give the answer that you want me to."
– *Oh Well* by Fleetwood Mac

"How you gonna win when you ain't right within?"
– *Doo Wop (That Thing)* by Lauryn Hill

"I'm starting with the man in the mirror,
I'm asking him to change his ways"
– *Man in the Mirror* by Michael Jackson

"Act your age mama, not your shoe size"
– *Kiss* by Prince

"Fly me to the moon and let me play among the stars. Let me see what spring is like on Jupiter and Mars."
– *Fly Me to the Moon* by Frank Sinatra

These lyrics take us back to fond memories. Maybe they touch a nerve around a painful memory. Lyrics can pick a side of a social issue or show support for those in need. We all connect with music in some way, and therefore, you can use music to connect when you converse. You can use a lyric like a quote, or you can you use it to initiate an idea.

As you begin to use some of these musical techniques you will notice they tie-in to physicality such as facial expression, body movement and other gestures. This was covered quite a bit in Chapter 4. Now, adding all this together becomes a bit of work. Know this–if you deliver a truly impactful message, it will feel like work. I heard once that a preacher's 30-minute sermon is the equivalent of an 8-hour day of work. Considering that, you should see conversation as an exercise, and what do we do prior to exercise? We warm up, and the same should be done to your conversation to make sure your entire being is ready to deliver your message.

Chapter 6

Communicating is Scary—Speak Anyway

"There is only one thing that makes a dream impossible to achieve: the fear of failure."
- *Paulo Coelho*

Do you know what the number one fear in the world is? It's not spiders, being attacked by a shark or falling. It's actually glossophobia, the fear of public speaking. Speaking is the thing that makes grown men and women dizzy and nauseous and children feel as though they may cry. The American Psychological Association identifies the varying levels of fear as ranging from low-level anxiety, like when your palms sweat before a big presentation, to phobia that might look like uncontrollable shaking even thinking about speaking at an event.[4]

When I was new to speaking, several thoughts would race in my mind before a presentation: *What will my listeners think of me? What will they think of what I have to say? Do they see all my physical flaws? Do they know more than I do about this topic? Am I qualified enough? Am I good enough? I can tell they don't like me.* These are all things I told and asked myself, and they were the worst possible thoughts. Yet, despite the negative thoughts, my hope was for a far more favorable outcome. I then expected others to feel positive about me and have great anticipation of what I had to say. The questions and self-doubts were rooted in fear. They impede your confidence and overburden you, limiting the great opportunities you have to positively impact the people in your life. Nevertheless, we often can't help it, the fear just seems to show up. What now?

To overcome fear and these self-defeating thoughts I often defer to prayer, meditation,

---

[4] Taken from the American Psychological Society, *How to Keep Fear of Public Speaking at Bay.*

visualization and affirmations. Most are familiar with prayer and meditation, often very personal as the approaches vary widely. However, visualization and affirmations can have a universal language. These will enable you to lessen your fears about communicating your ideas.

I like to imagine that the crowd is expecting to hear great things from me. They will love what I have to say. They will want more when I'm done. They respect me and my craft. They look at me as a person of substance who has their best interests at heart. After thinking all these good thoughts, I then say aloud, "I am good enough. I am capable and talented. We are going to enjoy each other's company for the next hour." Speaking these words *audibly,* I cancel out the internal fear talk that plays out in my mind. Don't worry about results, let them take care of themselves. You should then be able to calm yourself and deliver your best message.

Fear does not have to be a deal breaker that prevents you from communicating your ideas with audiences of any size. Ask public or professional speakers, and they will agree that the fear and nerves are always there and never fully leave you. Getting up in front of a group, no matter the size, can be intimidating. Most speakers, no matter how accomplished, have the initial fear of getting up in front of people. Speaking up brings the attention to you at a time when it may be easier to blend in.

The difference between the novice and the accomplished communicator is that somewhere on the journey to becoming a better speaker, the professional learns that fear is not a stop sign.

Speaking doesn't paralyze the accomplished communicator from taking a step forward. They still get sweaty palms, feel like they may lose their lunch, forget one of their major points, or make a fool of themselves. Their knees shake, a cold sweat ensues, and anxiety grips them. If a speaker can internalize that these are the symptoms of fear *without* allowing the fear to overwhelm them in the moment, fear can be a powerful tool.

Work with Your Fear, Not Against It

Early in my career, I became accustomed to speaking in front of groups of people as part of my job. I had nerves and doubts like everyone else, but I never saw fear as a reason to waver. I just went for it. Over the years, I've learned that overcoming the fear of speaking in public is one thing but being ready to speak in front of a group of people was another level altogether.

Adding value and involving the audience are necessary parts in your role as a communicator. You have to be able to move past your fear in order to connect with your listeners.

Work through your fear with these simple steps:

1. Use positive self-talk.
2. Do what you can where you are.
3. Step out of your comfort zone
4. Plan for the best possible outcome.

Revisit these steps as you grow in your communication skills. You will find that they can be beneficial at different stages in your process.

Use Positive Self-Talk

Words have power. When you share kind words with friends and loved ones, you are speaking truth into their lives. Your generosity and benevolence to others will return to you. Likewise, the way you speak to yourself will directly impact your abilities.

"Realize that you will never, on a sustained basis, exceed your own self-image because it serves as an invisible ceiling, and your self-image is determined by your inner dialogue," writes Sara J. White, M.S., FASHP[5]. She goes on to add, "Your feelings are an indication of your self-talk. If you are feeling unenergetic, down, or like you cannot face the world, switch to self-talk that is positive. Try telling yourself phrases such as, *"It is going to be a great day,"* and *"I am going to be successful today!"* Your feelings will change because you are focusing on the positive. Positive expectations tend to become reality, so use your feelings as a barometer of inner dialogue and change it when necessary.

What is your self-image as a communicator? Do you know where you are in the process of becoming a better communicator? Everyone is on their own journey to perfect their craft. Use positive language when reviewing your performance, especially when you pinpoint areas which need work.

---

[5] Fellow of the American Society of Health System Pharmacists.

Do What You Can Where You Are

We all started somewhere. The best way to work through your fear of speaking is to take small steps toward your long-term goal. Do what you can with the experience you already have as you continue to develop your skills. You may surprise yourself. I know in the instances when I pushed myself to show up before I thought I was ready, wonderful things have happened. Don't believe me? Wait until you hear how I met my wife.

When I first met the woman, who would become my wife, I was extremely quiet with very little to talk about. I fashioned myself on being the strong, silent type. After some time, I realized all that my silence was going to get me was alone. I had every opportunity. There was the time on the elevator, I said nothing. Passing each other in the quad, I said nothing. I must have had a hundred opportunities and said nothing. Finally, on a Valentine's Day afternoon in the lunchroom, I walked up to a table where she was sitting with several friends, handed her a card and said, "Happy Valentine's Day." Yes, I mustered up the courage to say those three words and that started a relationship that was worth every bit of dread I had.

A few years later, I took the Myers-Briggs Type Indicator along with a couple of other tests, and they described me as an introvert. That identifier helped me understand why I was withdrawn most of the time, and I discovered I can learn to be more interactive by process. I learned to be more communicative and how to have something to talk about. The best part? You can learn how to do those things too. Although I am not naturally talkative like others, I have learned to be talkative by preparing myself with ready-to-go content. Your potential for speaking engagements and your success in conversations each center around your ability to be comfortable with what you know and competent at delivering that knowledge. It doesn't matter what you don't know at that point. What you do know is key and how you bring it to life based on your experiences makes all the difference in the world.

Step Out of Your Comfort Zone

When I started my career, I was an accountant. This was perfect for my natural preference toward being quiet because I didn't have to interact too much, and I literally had my face in a ledger for most of the day. My go-to state of being would soon take a shift out of my comfort zone. Shortly after I started my career, I was asked to supervise my team. When I heard the offer, I wasn't sure what all the new responsibilities would be, but I knew I could use the promotion and increase in pay, so I accepted.

After a couple weeks my boss came by and said, *"Derek, you have to speak to your team."* I was confused. Didn't they know what they needed to do? My boss agreed that, yes, in general, the team knew what was needed. He prompted that I should set the priorities for the team and inquire how each was doing. Based on that info, I could set a strategy for them. I was shocked. How naïve of me! I wanted to shrink back and hide in my ledger again but instead I said, *"I understand."*

After some thought, I decided I would start small and go from there. The next day I made a point to stop at each staff member's desk and say good morning. I'd ask specifically if they needed anything. I supervised approximately 30 associates, so by the fifteenth desk I was shaking in my boots and feeling pretty drained. Not to mention, everyone could hear everyone else's questions.

If speaking one-on-one was nerve-wracking, the thought of presenting to a group of 30 would cause me to collapse. A month into the process, I felt a little more at ease with the one-on-ones and began to notice other things about my team. They had families, they had other interests; there were places and ideas around which we could connect. It was taking longer and longer to conduct this daily walk around and, for the sake of time, I needed to get the team together as a larger group.

Plan for the Best Possible Outcome

As a new manager of the accounting department, I was reluctant to speak to my team as a group. I wanted to hide when it was time to give new directives or ask for input on an upcoming project. Instead of allowing myself to wallow in my fear, I struck out to set myself up for success.

I went from desk to desk thinking that the best possible outcome was that I would communicate better with my team. I gave myself a pep talk and reminded myself that I can take these small steps to become a better communicator. In doing so, I became a more confident leader, and a confident leader automatically brings more value to the team. The positive self-talk helped, but combined with the positive vision, I received the change-producing outcome that worked for me.

Positive self-talk is important, but it isn't enough on its own to keep your [speaking] progress moving forward. To create the energy to follow through on your thoughts, you also need to think of your current situation in the best possible light. That means if you are a new speaker, you appreciate the knowledge you have and recognize that you have more to learn. A good mantra that's worked for me is *I'm always learning.*

Describing your situation in the best light means when someone asks you how the speaking thing is going, you tell them the truth. You tell them your recent wins and what you are working toward. Frame your current status in a favorable way and mention the opportunities you would like to come your way. When you are kind to yourself about where you are in your journey, you allow others the opportunity to cheer you on.

As you explain what you have achieved so far and invite others to share in your joy, people will be drawn to you. Your excitement about communicating and engaging will influence how they describe you to others. You never know when a kind word from the right person will launch your speaking experience to the next level. Just as you need to exhibit your true personality and kindness at each interaction, you can plan for the best possible outcome every time you have the opportunity to speak.

When you focus on improving specific public speaking skills you can overcome the fear and rid yourself of the paralysis that keeps you from sharing your unique value with others. We all have value to add to the world–some in a classroom, some in their families, some in politics, some in comedy, some as a motivational speaker. No matter what walk of life or chosen profession, you can help people by not just moving past your fear of speaking, but by being a well-prepared speaker. Working to become a polished communicator will aid you in ensuring that you deliver the best speech possible and that your listeners receive the most value from your contribution.

Chapter 7

Recognize Opportunities to Speak

"Thousands of geniuses live and die undiscovered - either by themselves or by others."

- *Mark Twain*

Now that you have started building your repertoire of endless content, tailoring and accessorizing, and fighting the fear, you should consider when you can start putting your skills to use. Through these last chapters, I have explained how you can *Say It Well* in many situations. Finally, I want to help you recognize opportunities when you can speak up and share your knowledge. Whether you are at work, at home, or in the community, you can provide value to the people around you. There are three steps you can use to recognize opportunities to speak and three main places to speak:

1. Find the people you need to associate with.
2. Bring your previous experience and your renewed enthusiasm.
3. Share your knowledge in a way that adds value.

Find the People You Need to Associate With

One of my favorite animated movies is *The Lion King*. Admittedly, I probably wouldn't have seen it if I didn't have kids, so I am thankful for its timing. The title song, *The Circle of Life*, has a passage that says, *"There's more to see than can ever be seen, more to do than can ever be done."* Similarly, there are more people to communicate with than can ever be communicated to.

You need to know the members of *your* target community. Who are the people most connected to your ideas, your interests, your information? If you find yourself talking, and nobody is listening, there is nothing wrong with you, you just haven't connected with *your* audience. Think about when you scan through the dial of radio stations every station doesn't apply to you. As you scan through you pass Rock, R&B, Hip-Hop, then– you find your favorite Country station, and you lock in. Likewise, you just need to keep moving until you lock in on your audience.

How do you find your audience?

Think about your interests. If you're into boating, find boating groups. If you are interested in public speaking, target groups such as Toastmasters or the National Speakers Association. If you are not connected to any groups, try out different hobbies, and you will begin to connect with people of similar interests, and your message will shine through.

I like to create music, so I have several acquaintances that love music as well. We like similar and dissimilar types of music, it doesn't matter which style we are enjoying in the moment. We spend a great deal of time talking about new music that is available. Indie artists are always out there creating new sounds and ideas for us to ponder and enjoy. We love sharing this commonality and sending texts with new finds from time to time. We have no roadblocks in our communication about music, it's the ideal – *locked in!* You will know you have found your audience if you are learning new things and growing as a person. Your audience will motivate you to be a better speaker and excel in other areas of your life as well.

Bring Your Previous Experience and Your Renewed Enthusiasm

Once I heard a pastor say, "We don't have the same history, but we share the same humanity." This reality rattled me and unlocked another truth: we all come from different walks of life and have very different experiences; however, they align across themes and modes. Despite the differences in experiences, we can share and add that value to each other's lives. Moreover, we can give each other support as we walk out our lives together. Given this, we can find the audiences that benefit most from our life's journey.

One of my daughters is a cancer survivor. This impacted each one of our family members differently, but my daughter was forever changed, and that change would go on to benefit others. She told her story, posted it on YouTube. It was therapeutic for her and will forever be a source of hope to others. She went on to speak to other organizations and help others that are experiencing journeys similar to hers. In this example, and please know that my daughter has been cancer free for 3½ years, her experience has led her to her audience. Let your experiences be your guide, and you will find your audiences that are ready to be influenced by how you dealt with the situation, your emotions and everything in between.

Moreover, my son, being a collegiate athlete, found a voice in helping young, aspiring athletes. When he was younger, he wanted to play sports and realized, as his talent grew, it wasn't all fun and games. There was a lot of practice and hard work required–early morning workouts, after school workouts, special diets– which meant he had to limit his favorite snacks and eat green vegetables. There were also the injuries, hospital visits and physical therapy. While all of this was going on, he also had to go to school and keep his grades up. If you talk to him now, he says it was well worth it. He goes back to the coaches that helped him when he was younger and helps inspire the younger kids coming up. He gives them confidence that they, too, can succeed by sharing his journey to becoming a college athlete. He has found his own unique audience.

My oldest daughter, who is an entrepreneur, communicates mainly on a one-on-one level. She has to effectively connect with her audience, potential clients, in order to appeal to their needs and make the sale. She has developed her niche in the marketplace that attracts a select group of customers. This audience holds her accountable for communications around articulating services that will be delivered in exchange for value. She has developed her communications and sales approach that ensures she reaches her intended audience every time.

Draw on your personal experiences, like my children have done. Share the stories with your audience that fire you up, the ones that bring a light into your eyes no matter how many times you retell it.

Share Your Knowledge in a Way That Brings Value

After the exercises in this book, I hope that you are confident in your knowledge and brave enough to share your stories. As you go into the community, post online, or even just comment at an office meeting. Keep in mind that the way you share content speaks volumes. Sharing knowledge with an audience that is unwilling or unable to receive will not help you, and it will definitely not help them. Focus on sharing from a place of giving and trust that the right listeners will come when they are meant to be there.

Say It Well . . .

- at the office.
- at home.
- in the community.

You are ready to *Say It Well,* and you could probably start doing it anywhere. It may be a better plan to strategize where, so you can communicate your best ideas in the best way. Remember the branching exercise where you listed your interests and areas of expertise. The places you can *Say It Well* tie in nicely with the structure of that exercise.

Say It Well **at the Office.**

Take, for example, the communication at your workplace. You would first outline the topics you might speak about at work. Notice anything unexpected? Yes, that's almost the exact same diagram from Chapter 1. You can use a new TOC–Tree of Content–to brainstorm ideas just by starting from a new branch. You can create overlap in each of these categories that you would normally have opportunities to communicate your ideas. For instance, when you talk to a colleague, you aren't just asking about deadlines and the next big project. You are talking about your favorite sports team and what show you watched on TV last night.

There is nothing wrong with casual conversation and it can serve as a great tool to strengthen relationships with your co-workers as well as within the organization. *Say It Well* gives you the confidence to bridge the gap between idle chatter and meaningful, informed dialogue. There are two common opportunities to communicate that you will want to keep in mind:

1. **Presentations.** Volunteer to present projects from your department. This is a way to stay top of mind among the company's leadership and contribute value to your team.

2. **Meetings.** Meetings are a low-risk way to practice explaining your ideas. Your audience is comprised of people you know, and you are presenting information that is readily at hand.

Leading conversations at work builds your reputation as a hard worker who is intelligent and ready to ascend the ladder.

Say It Well at Home

Your family and friends see you at your best and your worst. Many people who are good communicators outside the home may struggle when communicating with their loved ones. There can be a disconnect between people with whom you have a long history.

When communicating at home, you can *Say It Well* by remembering to speak in ways that *add value*. For family, the value could be a kind word to a young child or a deep discussion with a spouse. I remember my mother telling me, "You can't un-ring a bell once it's gone off." At the time, I had no clue what she meant, but now I know that she means that once words leave your mouth, they can't be unsaid. Choose your words carefully and make sure they are ones that align with your values and goals. If you are a parent, be an example to your children of the ways to add value to a conversation.

Here are a few exercises you can practice with people of all ages:

- **20 Questions**. Instead of one person answering 20 yes-or-no questions, encourage each member of the family to envision the future— share a story of what they think people will ask each other in twenty years. Respond with your best imaginative story.

- **Topic of the Night.** When planning for a meal together, allow the cook to choose the topic of discussion for the evening. Some families may even enjoy making the night into a themed party.

- **Review of each day.** Start a ritual with your loved ones where you close the day with a highlight of the best or worst moments. Encourage each other to talk about a challenge and how they plan to address it.

Say It Well in the Community

The world is waiting! You are ready to head out and share your thoughts and ideas with the great beyond. Whether you find yourself on the board of your HOA, your local non-profit organization or local club, your communication skills will be a big asset.

You can *Say It Well* each and every day by thinking about topics before you leave your home. Stay informed on the issues that are important to you and are affecting your community. Keep reading and growing as a person. The more you know, the more information and experience you will be able to add to a conversation or speech. Engaging with a community offers a lot of opportunities to get involved in your favorite projects. You can search online at sites like MeetUp for the types of clubs that meet near you. If you live near a larger city, you can find hundreds of options. Keep trying until you find the people you need to meet.

Practice *Say It Well* in your:
- Local libraries,
- Professional organizations
- Religious institutions.

Share your ideas and journey. Listen for gems of content you can add to your repertoire. People are waiting to hear your story from the person who knows it best—You! Never forget: you are a well of endless content. And now that you can *Say It Well*, your audience will be saying, "Well said!"

References

10 Most Common Reasons for Divorce. (2018, September 18). Retrieved from https://www.marriage.com/advice/divorce/10-most-common-reasons-for-divorce/

Florida A&M University. (n.d.). Retrieved from http://www.famu.edu/index.cfm?a=marching 100

How to Keep Fear of Public Speaking at Bay. (n.d.). Retrieved from https://www.apa.org/monitor/2017/02/tips-sidebar.aspx

National Pony Express Association. (n.d.). Retrieved from https://nationalponyexpress.org/

Valvano, J. (n.d.). Jimmy Valvano ESPY Awards Speech 1993. Retrieved from https://academyatthelakes.org/wp-content/uploads/2016/02/JimValvanoESPYAwardSpeech1993Excerpts.pdf

Acknowledgements

And as he entered into a certain village, there met him ten men that were lepers, which stood afar off: And they lifted up their voices, and said, "Jesus, Master, have mercy on us. " And when he saw them, he said unto them, "Go shew yourselves unto the priests." And it came to pass, that, as they went, they were cleansed. And one of them, when he saw that he was healed, turned back, and with a loud voice glorified God, and fell down on his face at his feet, giving him thanks: and he was a Samaritan. And Jesus answering said, "Were there not ten cleansed? But where are the nine?" They were not found that returned to give glory to God, save this stranger. And he said unto him, "Arise, go thy way: thy faith hath made thee whole." – Luke 17:11-19 (NIV)

      This is one of my favorite passages of scripture. It demonstrates the power of gratitude. I wish I had encountered it early in life, but I'm glad I had the opportunity to learn it in my lifetime. I know throughout my journey there have been numerous people who have taught me something, shown me grace when I didn't deserve it, and offered me a helping hand in times of need. I'm sure I obliged the gesture, and if not, please know I would return today and show my sincerest appreciation for what you have contributed to what is now my life to this point.

My mother always wanted the best for me, and I imagine she is cheering me on even today. She has physically been apart from me for more than 25 years, but her presence is as close as ever. I see her in me, in my children, and in the hopes and dreams that I pursue. I have been passed a baton to carry forward and pass to my children. This baton ascertains a better way forward for the next generations, and I would be remiss not to mention the care that my grandparents gave me. They filled in often when mom could not carry the burden alone.

The family that I am privileged to serve each and every day own my smile, my laughter and my heart. There is not a day that I don't think of the welfare of my wife and kids. I am so thankful that I have been able to provide for them and add some value to their lives. They have paid it back in spades, and I am eternally grateful for their love.

Over the last three decades, I have built my professional identity, and so many people have had a hand in that development. My managers, co-workers, and vendor partners at Motorola stay in my thoughts as I build on the foundation they have helped to establish. The same can be said of my family at Winn-Dixie; there I met folks that have taught me, and those who have allowed me to impose on them my theories, many of which have been refined here.

The friends that I have kept close from high school and all the friends I have met along the way I am extremely appreciative for your companionship. I have met some incredible people in the world of Toastmasters. They have helped me understand how to think about the value that I can deliver to the world through my ideas and the skills I have acquired over a long career.

I truly believe there are no accidents, and God has a plan for all of us. I am grateful for faith for it has enabled me to believe beyond myself and hope for the betterment of us all.

About the Author

Say It Well is Derek Lott's authorial debut. Lott has been speaking on the subject of communication as part of his personal and professional development methodology that he has been perfecting over 20 years. A career veteran of the high-tech and retail grocery industries, Lott has chosen to capture his effective philosophies for a broader audience.

Lott has spoken to various audiences from academia to industry to community. To help him further hone his skills, he joined a Toastmasters club in 2013. After completing the curriculum, Lott identified how he could help others improve their speaking skills. Thus, the creation of *Say It Well*, the proven approach to developing, organizing and tailoring content for any given audience.

Lott lives in Florida with his wife of 28 years. Together, they have three children.